The Spirit

How Renewal is Breaking Down Barriers
between Evangelicals and Roman Catholics

Peter Hocken

GROVE BOOKS LIMITED
RIDLEY HALL RD CAMBRIDGE CB3 9HU

Contents

1. A New Situation 3
2. Issues and Challenges 6
3. Israel as Catalyst 14
4. Towards a New Methodology for Evangelical-Catholic Encounter 21

The Cover Illustration is by Peter Ashton

Copyright © Peter Hocken 2001

First Impression July 2001
ISSN 1470-8531
ISBN 1 85174 471 1

1
A New Situation

This booklet addresses the relationship between Evangelical Christians and Roman Catholics. It argues that in the last thirty years momentous changes have been taking place that make both possible and desirable a new chapter in Evangelical–Catholic relations.

The new factor that has made possible a new relationship is the charismatic movement, and in particular its surprising outbreak in the Roman Catholic Church. In the charismatic renewal, there is for the first time in Christian history a spiritual awakening that has been affecting the Catholic as well as the Protestant world, not only penetrating the Roman Catholic Church, but also being welcomed and affirmed by the Catholic hierarchy, especially by the popes.

The present time as we begin the third millennium is perhaps a moment of unprecedented opportunity for a new and positive chapter in Evangelical–Roman Catholic relations. Two major changes have already taken place that favour a new relationship. First, the Second Vatican Council (1962–65) committed the Catholic Church in communion with Rome to a renewal that emphasized a return to the biblical sources and encouraged Catholics to read the Bible, to a renewal of Catholic worship that included the use of vernacular languages, and that recognized the work of the Holy Spirit in other Christian traditions. Only fifteen months later the Catholic charismatic renewal began in Pennsylvania and quickly spread around the world. Before this opening up from traditional Roman Catholic exclusiveness, it would have been unthinkable that the Catholic leadership could receive and welcome a movement that had its origins in the Protestant world.

Secondly, it is in the last fifteen to twenty years that the Evangelical world has opened up to the charismatic impulse. In the 1960s, the fiercest opponents of the newly-emerging charismatic movement were the Evangelicals. They saw great dangers in this new phenomenon, particularly of subordinating the word of God to subjective experience. Their fear of irrationality fuelled their opposition to speaking in tongues. (Interestingly, Roman Catholic responses to the charismatic renewal never expressed any difficulties with the gift of tongues.) A major change in Evangelical attitudes to the charismatic was already evident in the worship at the Lausanne II conference in Manila in 1989 by comparison with Lausanne I in 1974. Among the factors promoting this charismatic penetration of Evangelicalism have been: the influence of John Wimber and the Vineyard movement, urging the practice of spiritual gifts without insisting on a doctrine of baptism in the Spirit; the steady spread of healing ministries; the church planting movement and the cell movement, both emphasizing every-member ministry; and in the 1990s the remarkable diffusion of the Alpha course.

Perhaps the prime symbol for the changed attitude of Evangelicals to Roman Catholics is Dr Jim Packer, whose credentials as a Bible-believing Evangelical scholar no-one could impugn. In the mid-1960s, Dr Packer was a leading Evangelical critic of the charismatic movement. In the 1980s, Dr Packer took part regularly in conferences defending historic Christian orthodoxy and promoting spiritual renewal, organized by the Word of God Community in Ann Arbor, Michigan, an inter-denominational community with a Catholic majority. His first-hand experience of charismatic Catholics led him to revise his views, both of the charismatic movement and of the Roman Catholic Church. In the 1990s, Dr Packer became one of the major Evangelical contributors to the initiative 'Evangelicals and Catholics Together' in the USA.

How Possible?

What is it about the charismatic movement that has made such an unexpected development possible? I would single out the following elements as major contributory factors:
- the evident similarity of the grace of baptism in the Spirit across the church spectrum;
- its christocentric character, perhaps the surest sign of the charismatic movement as a true work of the Holy Spirit. It has constantly exalted Jesus, manifested his lordship, insisted on his ministry of full salvation;
- its rootedness in the Scriptures. While the renewal has not always favoured rigorous and scholarly attention to the biblical text, it has been a Bible-loving movement, often encouraging an attention to biblical books neglected in more doctrinally-focused circles;
- the new features in charismatic renewal—spiritual gifts, healing, prophetic words, simultaneous praise—all have a biblical basis;
- finally, and most importantly, the charismatic movement has been rooted first in an experience of the Lord in the Spirit, and not on a particular set of doctrines. This has made possible the reception of this blessing of God in any Christian body confessing Jesus as Lord and Saviour and the Holy Spirit as the giver of life.

Pioneer Developments

As a result of the outpouring of the Spirit in the charismatic renewal, several remarkable developments have taken place in Evangelical-Catholic relations, which indicate the new possibilities opened up by the Holy Spirit.

The Roman Catholic-Pentecostal Dialogue. This was the first new initiative made possible by the charismatic renewal spreading to the Roman Catholic Church. Though in its initial phase more important for the fact of its existence than for its achievements, more recently this dialogue has produced the important report on *Evangelization, Proselytism and Common Witness* (1998).

Italy. An important development has taken place in Italy arising from the personal friendship between a Catholic layman prominent in the Catholic charismatic renewal, Matteo Calisi of Bari, and a Pentecostal pastor, Giovanni Traettino of Caserta. Since 1992, Calisi and Traettino have held an Evangelical-Catholic conference each year with a Catholic and a Pentecostal speaker, and they have witnessed together on reconciliation in many nations, including France, the Czech republic and Northern Ireland.

Evangelicals and Catholics Together (ECT). This North American initiative came from several leading scholars convinced of the importance of Evangelicals and Catholics working together to defend traditional Christian orthodoxy and moral standards in the face of increasing decline, particularly in the witness of the mainline Protestant churches. The original statement entitled *Evangelicals and Catholics Together: The Christian Mission in the Third Millennium* (1994) was prepared by fifteen scholars and endorsed by twenty-five church leaders. The ECT initiative has continued, leading to a second document *The Gift of Salvation* (1997).

Evangelical Catholic Initiative (ECI). ECI is a Roman Catholic initiative in Ireland of a group calling themselves 'Evangelical Catholics' coming largely from lay circles in the Catholic charismatic renewal. A leaflet 'What is an Evangelical Catholic?' seeks to demonstrate the compatibility of basic Evangelical convictions with renewed Roman Catholic faith. ECI has proved to be a significant force for Evangelical-Catholic reconciliation in Ireland, promoting joint prayer breakfasts and repentance initiatives, as well as producing *Evangelicals and Catholics Together in Ireland*, an Irish revision of the American document.

Alpha. Another major force for Evangelical-Catholic rapprochement has been the Alpha course from the Anglican parish of Holy Trinity, Brompton in London. Since the course was made public in 1993, Alpha has spread all over the world and is being used by most Christian churches. It has won surprising acceptance among Catholics, and several hundred Roman Catholic parishes in Britain are known to have run Alpha courses.

Austria. In Austria, Christians from many denominations have formed *Weg der Versöhnung* (Way of Reconciliation). It gathers leaders from an unprecedented range of churches and movements, including Evangelicals, Pentecostals, free church charismatic, pietistic and charismatic Lutherans and representatives from Catholic renewal movements. They organized a 'Feast for Jesus' in Stephansplatz, the square outside St Stephen's Cathedral in Vienna, in June 2001.

2
Issues and Challenges

Most Christians probably think that there are insuperable doctrinal obstacles in the way of any effective rapprochement or extensive collaboration between Evangelicals and Roman Catholics. Evangelicals typically see themselves as true 'Bible-believers' and the Catholic Church as unbiblical. Catholics typically see their church as the one true church of Christian history and Evangelicals as fundamentalists imbued with an individualistic spirit that has no understanding of the church.

In order to get beyond these stereotypes, we need to look at the major areas of contention and difficulty, to see where the typical Catholic and Evangelical emphases may be complementary rather than opposed, and where both have a biblical foundation. We will then look at ways in which the Pentecostal and charismatic movements have been contributing or have a potential to contribute to less polarized positions.

Gospel and Mystery

As a starting point, I have chosen two key concepts that are not a major point of contention, but which nonetheless are in some way the glory of each camp. *Gospel* is the glory of the Evangelicals, representing the good news of salvation, the truth that sets the believer free, the core of Evangelical faith. *Mystery* represents the glory of the Catholic faith, the celebration today in powerful symbols of the great acts of God, the awesome presence of the Incarnate Lord, that cannot be reduced to mere words.

In fact, both terms are biblical. The gospel is above all the news of an event—the good news of the resurrection. 'We bring you the good news that what God promised to the fathers, this he has fulfilled to us their children by raising Jesus' (Acts 13.32–33). But this event has immense significance; it is the message of salvation. 'For I am not ashamed of the gospel; it is the power of God for salvation to everyone who has faith, to the Jew first and also to the Greek' (Rom 1.16). This message has to be proclaimed; the risen Jesus tells his disciples: 'Go into all the world and preach the gospel to the whole of creation' (Mark 16.15). Peter and John were 'preaching the gospel to many villages of the Samaritans' (Acts 8.25). Paul's call is to 'preach the gospel' (1 Cor 1.17; 2 Tim 1.11), which is to preach Christ (see Gal 1.16). Here we can see three major Evangelical themes associated with the term 'gospel': the cross and resurrection of Jesus; the message of salvation; and the necessity of proclamation.

Mystery in the Scriptures means above all the eternal plan of God hidden throughout the ages but now revealed by Christ through his Spirit to the saints. This description draws upon Rom 16.25–26 ('kept secret for long ages but…now disclosed'), Eph 3.5 ('not made known…in other generations as it has now been revealed to the holy apostles and prophets by the Spirit'), and Col 1.26 ('the mystery hidden for ages and generations but now made manifest to his saints').

Mystery seems more comprehensive than gospel. Mystery refers to the indwelling of Christ, 'Christ in you, the hope of glory' (Col 1.27), to the admission of Gentiles to join Jews in the one new person that is Christ's body (Eph 2.15; 3.4–6), to the hardening of unbelieving Israel and their eventual admission (Rom 11.25) and to the resurrection of the last day (1 Cor 15.51).

The charismatic experience has reinforced the importance of gospel, providing a new impulse for evangelism (the Evangelical term) or for evangelization (the Catholic term). But it can also lead to the rediscovery of mystery, particularly in the inspiration of corporate praise and the exercise of spiritual gifts. The charismatic working of the Holy Spirit leads the worshipping community into experience of the ineffable that wonderfully transcends the limitations of more rationally-dominated forms of Protestant worship.

Spirit and Body

Both Evangelicals and Catholics believe that God is the creator of the spiritual and the bodily, that the human person is made up of spiritual and bodily elements. We both believe that the salvation of God in Christ extends to the whole person. Our salvation will only be complete with the resurrection of the body to share in the glory of the risen Lord. But Evangelicals and Catholics have distinctly different attitudes to the spiritual and the bodily.

Evangelicals are typically suspicious of all outward religion, especially of any ritual, which by definition involves ceremonies of a bodily nature. Catholics have been characterized by outward gestures and ceremonies—making the sign of the cross, genuflecting in church, wearing a cross or a medal. Evangelicals have a traditional fear of formalism, of any form of hypocrisy where outward practice does not spring from a renewed heart. For Catholics, outward practice is a natural expression of inner beliefs.

In the same way, Evangelicals have been loath to attribute any grace-producing effects to ministerial rites and gestures. Ceremonies prescribed by the Lord Jesus, such as baptism and the Lord's supper, are normally regarded as 'mere symbols.' They are seen as expressing something that has already happened in the realm of the Spirit. Evangelicals are suspicious of sacramental thinking that holds specific ritual actions to be instruments for the conveying of God's grace.

By contrast, Catholics believe that the sacraments are divinely-given instruments for imparting Christ's life to the church. Catholics see sacramental actions as in continuity with the Incarnation, in which the Word of God took on human flesh to be the instrument of God's salvation.

The Pentecostal and charismatic movements can be of great help in the overcoming of this spirit-body dichotomy. For the work of the Lord through baptism in the Spirit has always had a physical dimension. Pentecostal and charismatic Christians are known for bodily expression in worship and ministry—for raising hands in praise, for clapping and dancing, for the miming of songs, for the laying on hands in ministry. However, Pentecostal-charismatic teaching has not paid enough attention to this aspect of their practice. As a result, we have rarely seen its potential for the overcoming of these long-standing oppositions.

In some ways, the so-called 'Toronto blessing' (or better, the 'Father's blessing') carried further this element of physical expression. People spoke of 'impartation,' meaning a communication of the Holy Spirit by gestures. I remember hearing Terry Virgo, the leader of the New Frontiers network of charismatic churches, preach at the Airport church in Toronto about impartation, saying he had never learned this idea in Bible college. As a Catholic listener, I found the idea of impartation very familiar, even though Catholics do not use that particular term. It fits readily with a Catholic understanding of the instrumentality of Jesus's humanity and the instrumentality of the essential gestures of the church that we call sacraments.

Individual Believer and Faith Community

Another obvious difference between Evangelicals and Catholics concerns the individual believer and the faith community. This contrast is again one of differences of mentality that influence how divine revelation is understood and lived.

Evangelical Christians focus on the faith-response of each believer to God's saving grace in Jesus Christ. So when they speak of justification by faith, they mean that the believer is justified by the Lord through his/her own faith in Christ. For Evangelicals, each believer must profess faith personally, each must repent for sin, each must experience conversion and the forgiveness of sins. Each believer has direct access to the Father in the Spirit. Each must develop his/her own faith by Bible reading and prayer, and each is expected to have his/her own witness to share with others.

Catholic Christians think of the church before thinking of self and one's own personal faith. When Catholics come to faith, they are accepting the faith of the church. In a healthy expression of Catholic faith, the church is not experienced as a distant or repressive authority, but as 'the household of the faith,' as a mother who cares for her children.

Evangelicals typically think of church after conversion and personal faith. In practice, they tend to decide which church to join as a subsequent issue to their decision about Jesus, about salvation and eternal life. In this view, believers are directly influenced by fellow believers as well as being directly touched by the Lord, but the church is not normally seen as instrumental in re-birth and conversion. By contrast, Catholics formed in their faith see the church as instrument of salvation, not just as fruit. Evangelization is seen as a work of the church, baptism as an act of the church, and the font where baptisms take place like the womb of the church.

How has the charismatic renewal affected these perceptions? Though the first experience of renewal is often a powerful individual experience of the Lord in the Spirit, it is clear that in the renewal the Lord has been giving a stronger sense of community and of the Holy Spirit forming the body of Christ. It is common charismatic teaching that the spiritual gifts are not just individual endowments, but are gifts for the upbuilding of the body. The Catholic charismatic renewal has seen the rise of many new communities; in many charismatic milieux, especially the new charismatic churches, there is a stronger sense of the need not just to win converts but to form new churches. These are ways in which the Holy Spirit is at work to overcome the inherited tensions between the individual believer and the faith community.

Divine Intervention and Human Mediation

Evangelical Christians emphasize God's direct action in people's lives in conversion, in conviction of sin and in revival. Pentecostal and charismatic Christians accentuate this direct action of God, extending it to the regular hearing of God's voice, to the exercise of spiritual gifts, to works of deliverance and healing.

Catholic Christians believe that God works through the instrumentality of the church. This instrumentality is manifested in church teaching, in church government and pastoral care, in the liturgy and the sacraments, in spiritual guidance and direction. This human mediation is particularly represented in the hierarchy of pope and bishops, and in the ordained ministry.

It is not that Evangelical Christians deny all human instrumentality in the work of God. The ministry of preachers and pastors is important in Evangelical life, and there is the role of the Bible as God's created instrument. Nor am I saying that Catholics reject any direct relationship between God and the individual believer. However, they have often focused on the impact of the direct relationship to God of outstanding believers, in contrast to Evangelical belief in the priesthood of all believers.

It is clear that very different paradigms operate in the Evangelical and the Catholic worlds. Evangelicals start with the model of God and the believer in direct relationship, while Catholics start with the model of the believer as part of the church that relates directly to God. Evangelicals understand pastoral ministry within the Evangelical paradigm, and Catholics see personal interaction with God in the context of the church as an hierarchically-organized community of faith. These two models produce different attitudes towards the discernment of words and messages from on high.

We find a similar contrast in our attitudes to history. For those who emphasize direct divine intervention, what matters most is the present intervention. Faith comes from the Holy Spirit, who is poured out from heaven. Christian history is not so directly relevant. But for those who emphasize the mediation of the church, history is of huge importance. The faith is not something that descends from heaven today, but an inheritance passed down from generation to generation from the time of the apostles.

What differences does charismatic renewal make to these emphases? At first sight, the charismatic movement reinforces the experience of immediate divine intervention. It easily leads to an increase of tension with church authorities. However, at a subsequent and more mature stage, this experience often gives way to a recognition of the need for all claims to direct divine revelation or inspiration to be tested by the faith community. Many charismatic groups have had bitter experience of the divisive and harmful effects of insistent claims that 'God told me…'

Many new charismatic assemblies and networks are now entering their second and even their third generation, there is a growing awareness of the need to transmit their experience of living faith to the next generation. This is making many leaders more open to recognize that it is necessary both to pray for heaven-sent revival and to be the instruments for transmission of teaching and nurture.

Word and Sacrament

The Protestant Reformation led to a sharp contrast between word and sacrament. The Protestants appealed to the Bible as the word of God to reduce the number of sacraments from seven to two or three, or in the more radical groups to reject the idea of sacrament altogether, some replacing it with the language of ordinances. In reaction, the Catholic Church of the Counter-Reformation emphasized even more strongly the centrality of the sacraments, and opposed the Protestant usage of the Bible. The Catholic Church still believed that the Bible was the word of God, but in reaction to the Reformation saw Bible reading as dangerous for ordinary Christians and only to be allowed for learned clergy. This contrast between word and sacrament was further accentuated with the Evangelical revivals of the eighteenth century. The Protestant emphasis on the preaching of the word led to the Evangelical emphasis on the necessity for each believer of a personal experience of re-birth and conversion. So we find today a sharp opposition between an Evangelical emphasis on individual conversion and the Catholic belief that regeneration occurs at baptism.

Has the charismatic renewal made any difference to these oppositions? I see two major ways in which charismatic renewal is making possible a new and healthier relationship between word and sacrament. The first concerns Catholics and the Bible. A break-through in Evangelical-Catholic relations has been made possible through the official encouragement at Vatican II of Bible reading by the Catholic laity. While conciliar decrees by themselves do not change the popular habits of centuries, they prepared for the fruit of charismatic renewal. For it is the charismatic renewal that is making avid Bible readers of millions of ordinary Catholics.

At the same time, the Catholic bishops at Vatican II taught the complementarity of word and sacrament. The renewal of the church's liturgy requires that every sacramental celebration begins with a celebration of the word of God. Catholic charismatic renewal is a major influence bringing the word to life in a way that produces vibrant liturgical celebrations. In this experience worshippers learn to express the inner presence of the Holy Spirit through the outward gestures of liturgical rite and symbol. We learn to experience our body as essential to our comportment before God. With this harmony of inner faith and outer expression, Evangelical Christians can often recognize that their traditional objections and suspicions concerning set forms no longer have the same force.

Freedom and Authority

Here too very different paradigms are at work as to how Evangelical Christians and Roman Catholic Christians regard and experience freedom and authority. Evangelicals see freedom, spiritual freedom, as a direct consequence of conversion and re-birth. Freedom in Christ is the birth-right of the Christian. Texts like 'you will know the truth, and the truth will make you free' (John 8.32) and 'For freedom Christ has set us free' (Gal 5.1) speak strongly to Evangelicals. Catholics traditionally—at least post-Reformation Catholics—have begun from authority, properly constituted authority, as foundational for all other virtues and blessings. Texts like 'He who hears you hears me, and he who rejects you rejects me' (Luke 10.16) and 'Obey your leaders and submit to them' (Heb 13.17) have been more cited by Catholics than by Protestants.

In many ways the Evangelicals have inherited the Calvinist sense of *soli Deo gloria* (to God alone be the glory) with its profound sense of the unique holiness and authority of God. Some would say that this sense is less strong among many Pentecostals and charismatics, for whom forms of familiarity with God have attenuated this awesomeness. From this background, there is often the suspicion that church authority constantly infringes on the authority of God.

Catholics by contrast see the authority of the church as reflecting and mediating the authority of God. Faith in the teaching authority (*magisterium*) of the church hierarchy in their view grounds the stability of Christian teaching and its power to resist the spirit of each age. They see this fidelity as a fulfilment of Jesus's words: 'I am with you always, to the close of the age' (Matt 28.20). Where Evangelicals typically see one of the greatest threats to Christian liberty in the abuse of church authority (and Catholicism as a form of ecclesiastical tyranny over the human conscience), Catholics tend to see private judgment (every believer his own pope) as a major threat to Christian order and the unity of the church.

Does a movement such as charismatic renewal have anything to contribute to the right relationship between freedom and authority? The first experience of renewal often produces an intoxicating sense of the freedom of the children of God. There is a new freedom to give praise to the Lord, a new freedom to speak of the things of the Lord, a new freedom from the fear of what others think. A new respect for authority is not the most obvious fruit of renewal in the Holy Spirit.

However, the emphasis upon spiritual gifts as endowments of the Spirit for the church can promote an awareness of church authority as another gift of the Lord. The discovery of spiritual gifts (1 Cor 12.8–10) can lead to the discovery of 'ministry-gifts' (Eph 4.11). This necessarily raises the issue of authority (authority of apostles, of prophets, of pastors, of teachers). Such a rediscovery without an anchoring in history can produce its own problems, as was seen in the Discipleship or Shepherding controversies of the 1970s.

Many Catholic messages concerning charismatic renewal have spoken of the institutional and the charismatic as both necessary within the church, and of both as gift (*charism*). In a powerful message in Brighton in 1991, the papal preacher, Fr Raniero Cantalamessa, developed this point in a way unusual for a Catholic, insisting that the charismatic comes first. The visible action of the Spirit gives rise to and requires the gift of authority, that also comes from the Spirit and is to be exercised in the Spirit.

Jesus Christ and the Virgin Mary

For Evangelical Christians, the Virgin Mary is a symbol of Catholic excess. She represents what for the Evangelical is the most problematic and the most unbiblical about Roman Catholicism. For Catholics, the absence of any feel for Mary among Evangelical Protestants is a symbol of barrenness, of a deficit in art, in humanity and in reality. For Roman Catholics, it is natural to speak of Jesus and Mary. Jesus and Mary belong together. For the Evangelical, the 'and' seems blasphemous. 'For there is one God, and there is one mediator between God and men, the man Christ Jesus' (1 Tim 2.5).

Here the opposition seems the sharpest, the emotions run highest, and the abyss between Evangelical and Roman Catholic appears the most impossible to bridge. The fact that charismatic Catholics do not abandon their devotion to Mary more easily leads Evangelicals and Pentecostals to question the authenticity of their Spirit-baptism than to re-think their own attitudes to the mother of Jesus. Experience suggests that this is not the best point at which to begin discussion.

Scripture and Tradition

There is a close link between Scripture and tradition and the equally disputed question of Scripture and church. To attribute any weight to tradition is to attribute weight to the church, because the tradition being revered is church tradition. The differences between Evangelical Protestant and Roman Catholic here cover several related issues: the relationship between the Bible and the church; the weight to be accorded to past declarations of the church; the relationship between what the Faith and Order Conference of Montreal (1963) called 'the Tradition' (the core life of the church handed down through the generations) and the 'traditions' (all the varied ways in which the Christian faith has been lived and expressed). But perhaps the most fundamental focuses on the question of authority: between Evangelicals for whom the Bible is their sole authority; and Catholics, for whom the apostolic succession of pope and bishops guarantees a living voice that speaks with the authority of the Lord.

Summary

I have presented a number of major issues that arise in the Evangelical-Catholic encounter. It will be noticed that these issues are not all questions of opposed doctrines; some concern different emphases and priorities, contrasting ways of thinking and behaving. The major differences can be expressed in terms of *contrasts*, of *tensions* and of *oppositions*. That is why I have ordered this section by moving from contrasts to tensions to oppositions.

This way of approaching Evangelical-Catholic issues takes us more directly to the roots of our differences. The points of greatest opposition are rooted in different ways of thinking, which arose out of different patterns of experience. To say this is not to reduce all truth-issues to socio-cultural conditioning. But living in total isolation and mutual suspicion produces a situation in which it becomes ever more difficult to understand one another.

The factors cited in Chapter One that are bringing Evangelicals and Catholics together in an unprecedented way require that we reflect on all the ways in which we have grown and developed differently in separation and opposition. Since the charismatic renewal has played a major role in making this new encounter possible, I have indicated some ways in which the charismatic experience is changing our perceptions. What this means for the future, I will address further in the final chapter.

3
Israel as Catalyst

Evangelical-Catholic rapprochement is inevitably a difficult enterprise, in which ancient sensitivities are easily disturbed and old controversies quickly rekindled. Both sides have their guardians and their watchdogs ready to cry 'Foul' at the slightest sympathy for the other party. Many Evangelicals fear that change in the Roman Catholic Church is merely cosmetic and that 'renewed' Catholics are renewed in spite not because of their church.

Is the Roman Catholic Church Really Undergoing Renewal?
It is the question of Israel that is providing both the deepest challenge and the deepest grounds for hope. I am using the term 'Israel' rather than 'the Jewish people' not just because it is simpler, but because it expresses more clearly the theological dimension of the Jewish people as the people of the irrevocable covenant. It also evokes the land of Israel, that is intrinsic to the faith of the Jewish people, though Israel in this context is not to be identified with the modern state created in 1948.

First of all, it is the question of Israel that has been bringing the Catholic Church to an unprecedented repentance. This Catholic repentance is of great significance for Evangelical-Catholic relations. The enormity of the Holocaust with the scientific extermination of six million Jews in 'Christian Europe' has been like a time-bomb in the modern Christian conscience. The first Catholic gesture was Pope John XXIII's elimination of the word 'perfidious' from the liturgy of Good Friday, which had spoken of 'the perfidious Jews.' Soon after, in 1965, the Second Vatican Council officially rejected any teaching that the Jewish people were guilty of deicide, that they were an accursed people, and that God's covenant with Israel had been abrogated on account of the Jewish rejection of Jesus as their Messiah. The challenge to the Catholic conscience was being heard.

However, almost thirty years passed before Pope John Paul II courageously proposed an explicit Catholic repentance for the sins of the past. This the pope did in 1994 in a document concerning the church's preparation for the new millennium, saying: 'Acknowledging the weaknesses of the past is an act of honesty and courage.' He presented this confession as essential for a purification of memories. If there is no repentance for the sins of the past, we are in danger of repeating them in the future. The pope focused on two particular areas for a Catholic repentance: sins against unity; and sins of violence committed in the name of truth.

These preparatory teachings led to the remarkable liturgy of repentance led by the Pope in St Peter's Basilica on 12th March, 2000. During this liturgy, leaders of the departments of the Roman *curia* expressed a confession for sins relating to their area of responsibility, for example: 'We confess the sins which have harmed the unity of Christ's body, the church; we have often resisted, condemned and fought one another; grant us reconciliation and full communion.' Two weeks later, the Pope travelled to Israel, where he revealed this humbler face of the church to the Jewish people, particularly at the Holocaust memorial museum at Yad Vashem and in his prayer at the Western (so-called 'wailing') Wall.

Why are these events of great significance for Evangelical-Catholic relations? First, they are without precedent in Catholic history. Here is the conclusive proof that something radical is happening in the Roman Catholic Church. The people who knew this in their bones were the Israeli Jews, who saw that something momentous had happened during the Pope's visit. Secondly, Evangelicals understand the necessity of repentance for real change. Though the Catholic Church set out officially on the road of renewal in the 1960s, it has taken thirty-five years for this opening to reach the decisive step of confession and repentance that represents a deep change of heart.

Thirdly, the Israel issue is foundational for Evangelical-Catholic relations because it confronts both sides with their sin. A Jewish context enables Evangelicals and Catholics to meet not just as long-standing opponents, but as repentant fellow-sinners. Both sides have been guilty of replacement teaching and the accompanying attitudes of contempt and prejudice. By replacement teaching I refer to this complex of related ideas: (i) the Jewish people rejected Jesus as their Messiah; (ii) therefore God has rejected the Jewish people as his chosen covenant people, and the covenant with Israel was abrogated; (iii) the church has taken the place of Israel as God's covenant people; (iv) the promises originally given to Israel no longer belong to the Jews, but to the church.

Israel and the Church

What difference has the charismatic movement made to the Israel issue? The short answer is 'The Messianic Jews.' The Messianic Jews are Jewish believers in Jesus who in the last thirty years have been forming Messianic assemblies or synagogues in the belief that there is no valid reason why Jews who come to faith in Jesus (Yeshua) as their Messiah have to abandon their Jewish identity and live as Gentiles.

While the Messianic Jews are not all charismatic, it was the impulse of newly-converted and 'Spirit-baptized' Jews, particularly through the 'Jesus movement' of the late 1960s and early 1970s, that launched the Messianic movement and that now characterizes the majority of Messianic assemblies—found especially in the United States, in Israel, in Russia and in the Ukraine.

The Messianic Jews confront all Christians with the question: 'What happened to the Jewish church of the origins?' However we read the history of the first four Christian centuries, it is clear that a huge change happened between the totally Jewish church of the first generation (Acts 1–9) and the church of the fourth century, that required Jewish converts to renounce their Jewish identity and cease all Jewish observance.

The separation of church and synagogue involved a mutual rejection. First, the synagogue excluded those who accepted Jesus as the Messiah. Then the church excluded any Jewish expression of faith in Jesus. The first schism post-Christ is the schism within Israel; the second is within the church.

This is the right place to introduce a repentance for the replacement mentality. For, however hard this is for the Jewish community to accept, the rejection of the Jewish people began with their rejection within the Christian church. If the church had retained the first place of the Jew and honoured it, replacement thinking could not have developed, and the Jews would not have been despised as a people rejected by God.

The Depth of the Challenge

The ongoing necessity for a Jewish expression of the church poses with a new force the question of the continuity and the discontinuity between the old covenant(s) and the new. There is in the New Testament a displacement of the centre from the earthly Jerusalem to the heavenly, resulting from the resurrection-ascension of Jesus the Messiah. There is the construction of a new temple that is his body (John 2.21). Nonetheless, the covenants and the call of Israel are irrevocable. And at the end, the heavenly Jerusalem comes down to earth for the wedding feast of the lamb (Rev 21).

It is in Romans 9–11 that Paul gives the clearest refutation of replacement thinking: (i) God has not rejected the Jewish people (11.1); (ii) the Jews who receive Jesus are 'a remnant, chosen by grace' (11.5); (iii) the Jews, who did not believe in Jesus, have not stumbled beyond recovery (11.11); (iv) their 'fulness' (11.12), their 'acceptance' (11.15), their 'salvation' (11.26) is foretold, and will be more 'riches for the Gentiles' (11.12) and 'life from the dead' (11.15); (v) 'the gifts and the call of God are irrevocable' (11.29); (vi) 'God has consigned all [Jew and Gentile] to disobedience, that he may have mercy upon all' (11.32).

It is within this wider context that we need to examine the challenges posed to all Christian traditions, particularly the Catholic and the Evangelical, by the abandonment of replacement teaching.

The Challenge to the Catholics

There is a challenge to the Catholic view of the early church and the age of the church fathers. The Israel issue indicates that this was not as golden an age as Catholics (and Orthodox) have imagined. In rejecting the replacement teaching and insisting that the covenant with Israel has not been revoked, the Catholic Church has implicitly admitted that something became distorted in the early church.

A re-reading of Ephesians 2 and 3 in the light of this issue raises the question of how the exclusion of the Jewish witness damaged the unity of the church as 'the one new person' made up of Jew and Gentile reconciled through the blood of the cross. This raises a further question for Catholics: to what extent did the loss of the Jewish church and the bi-polar character of the foundation in Ephesians 2 make possible too political a view of the unity of a church closely bound to the Roman Empire?

The Challenge to the Evangelicals

The major challenge to the Evangelicals concerns the degree to which they have imbibed the replacement thinking. It can be put like this: the replacement thinking applied by the early church to Israel has been continued in every subsequent separation. So at the Reformation, the Reformers were saying: God has rejected the Catholic Church because of its corruption. God has raised us up to be the true church of the gospel. Thus, we have taken the place of the Catholics and the promises given to the church now belong to us. Later, some Christians concerned with revival of spiritual life left the Anglican, Lutheran and Reformed churches in disillusionment, using the same arguments: You are dead, you have betrayed the gospel. God has raised us up. We are now the authentic church.

Replacement thinking is a sin of arrogance and a denial of the mercy of God. Replacement thinking usurps God's unique role as judge. When Christians say of another body, of those marked in any way by God's covenant, 'God has rejected you,' they set themselves up as judge in the place of God. They fail to understand the mercy of God. When they regard themselves as the remnant and equate that with the true church, they fail to understand the biblical concept of the remnant that always remained but a part—the faithful part—of the chosen people.

It is important to see precisely where our sin lies. Only the Holy Spirit can truly convict us. There is no sin in believing that corruption in the church is an abomination in the sight of the all-holy God. There is no sin in believing that God punishes sin and rebellion. The sin lies in the absolute judgment: that God has rejected this people, that they have no more significance in God's sight.

We can see here how the Israel issue challenges both Catholics and Evangelicals at their point of greatest pride—in their self-understanding. To admit that something serious went wrong at an early stage in the history of the church strikes at the Catholic pride in *tradition*. The tradition has not been as pure as Catholics thought. To admit that they have been major victims of replacement thinking strikes at the Evangelical pride in being truly *biblical*. Evangelicals have not been as biblical as they thought.

Light on the Disputed Issues

We can now ask what light the Israel question throws on the issues examined in chapter 2. Perhaps Evangelicals and Catholics can agree that the way ahead lies in all becoming more biblical, in all returning more deeply to our common sources in the Scriptures. But the Israel issue indicates that an authentic return to the Scriptures must be a return to the roots in Israel.

This biblical renewal has then to purify our theology and our practice of every trace of replacement thinking. So in the Old Testament, we should understand 'Israel' (we/us, my people) to refer to 'Israel' first, and not immediately apply it to ourselves and the church. For example: 'Son of man, these bones are the whole house of Israel.' (Ezek 37.11); 'he was cut off out of the land of the living, stricken for the transgression of my people.' (Is 53.8).

What will we find when we look at the listed points of contrast, tension and opposition between Evangelicals and Catholics in the light of the life and the Scriptures of Israel? It is important to recognize that the Scriptures of Israel are not limited to the Old Testament, but that the New Testament is also predominantly a Jewish work. Of the issues described in Section Two, some are already found in the Old Testament (spirit and body, divine initiative and human mediation, Scripture and tradition); others exist in a preliminary form in the Old Testament but receive a clear expression only in the New Testament (word and sacrament, gospel and mystery). In these five instances, the Catholic-Evangelical oppositions of the last 250 years are not to be found in the Scriptures.

Spirit and Body

In the story of creation in Genesis 2, we find the composite nature of the human person clearly expressed. 'The Lord God formed man (*adam*) of dust from the ground, and breathed into his nostrils the breath of life; and the man became a living being.' (Gen 2.7). It is sin that introduces division, with the ultimate penalty of death, the separation of body and 'breath of life,' so that 'you are dust, and to dust you shall return' (Gen 3.19).

Here we find the fundamental reason why for the people of Israel, salvation will only truly come with the resurrection of the body. Salvation means the deliverance from all evil (sin, Satan, death) in God's creation. So Israelite-Jewish faith has always been very earthy. We find this expressed in Paul's teaching on the resurrection: 'But it is not the spiritual which is first but the physical, and then the spiritual.' (1 Cor 15.46). Above all, we find the total harmony of spirit and body in the sacrifice of Jesus, by which we are saved.

The spirit, the heart, the mind of Jesus are totally given to the Father through the offering of his body.

Divine Initiative and Human Mediation

Throughout the history of Israel, we find divine initiatives, acts of God's sovereign intervention in the life of his people—the call of Abraham, the deliverance from Egypt, the theophany of Sinai, the call of the prophets, the election of David and of Jerusalem. However, these divine interventions enter deeply into Israel's history. They ground Israel's liturgical celebrations, they give rise to the institutions of Israel's life as a people. The people sovereignly constituted as God's own are commanded to hand on the memories, the terms of the covenant, the rites and the laws, to each succeeding generation.

The rise of institutions, the formation of traditions, does not exclude further divine interventions. The history of Israel is a history of rebellion and of repentance, a history of ancient memories and of new beginnings, a history that combines the priestly, the kingly or governmental, and the prophetic. The coming of the Messiah involves greater divine intervention—above all in the Incarnation itself, in the virgin birth, and in the resurrection of Jesus—but they all enter into history and transform it.

Scripture and Tradition

The Israel issue can help Evangelicals to see the necessity of a respect for tradition. For the Jewish people are by definition the sons and daughters of Abraham, bound to God by historic covenants that are renewed and passed down from generation to generation. The formation of the canon of Scripture shows the consciousness in Israel and the church of the primacy of those writings regarded as sacred Scripture. But the formation of the canon took place in a context of great respect for the heritage of the people of God.

Word and Sacrament

In the Scriptures there is no opposition between the word and ritual action. Yes, there are protests against hypocritical outward lip-service. But Israelite-Jewish worship (until the destruction of the temple) always involved the proclamation of the Scriptures and the celebration of actions prescribed in the Scriptures. The Jews had a strong concept of *memorial*, seen especially in their observance of Passover. The command of Jesus to 'Do this in memory of me' was totally in line with the Israelite/Jewish heritage of ritual commemoration of saving events. With the biblical renewal in the Catholic Church, there is a fresh understanding of the eucharist as the memorial that makes present but does not repeat the unique sacrifice of the Lord.

Gospel and Mystery

Although both are New Testament terms whose meaning comes from their relationship to Jesus Christ, we can find in the later period of the Old Testament the same contrast between the major events of Israel's history (the deliverance from Egypt, the Sinai covenant, the entry into the promised land) and the first attempts to formulate a sense of God's plan from before all ages. There is a natural movement from the 'mighty acts of God' to the 'mystery' of God's plan. In this movement the Holy Spirit opens up the future God has for his chosen people, the eschatological hope.

Of the other issues, that between the *Individual Believer and Faith Community* undergoes a major transformation with the coming of the Messiah and the outpouring of the Holy Spirit. For it is a characteristic of the new covenant that each believer becomes a temple of the Holy Spirit (1 Cor 3.16) and that each has 'the anointing that abides' (1 John 2.27). However, it is clear from the whole New Testament that this new privilege of each believer does not weaken or destroy the strong collective sense that characterized the life of Israel. The letter that says the body of each believer is a temple of the Holy Spirit is the letter that gives the first detailed teaching about the church as the body of Christ. 'Now you are the body of Christ and individually members of it' (1 Cor 12.27). The comparison with the members of the human body indicates the organic character of this belonging. Parallel observations can be made concerning the issue of *Freedom and Authority* in the New Covenant.

What can be said about the difficult issue of Jesus and Mary? First, that many problems concerning Mary both in theology and in piety have arisen from her being separated from her proper context in relation to Israel and to Zion. In Revelation 12 'the woman clothed with the sun' (v 1) who 'brought forth a male child' (v 5) is first Zion and Israel; but in line with the biblical pattern of thought, the woman is also Mary, the personal embodiment of the people's calling. This chapter more than hints at the process whereby through the Messiah, Israel is transformed into the church, the offspring of the woman who 'keep the commandments of God and bear testimony to Jesus' (v 17). Secondly, we must not be prevented from seeking to relate rightly by the size of the obstacles. Is it not possible that the most difficult questions constitute the greatest challenge and contain the greatest potential blessings?

4
Towards a New Methodology for Evangelical-Catholic Encounter

If more positive relations are to develop between Catholics and Evangelicals, we need a clearer understanding of how to relate to one another. We need a new methodology for this important and necessary encounter. The elements or principles for such a methodology can be drawn from the preceding sections of this booklet. I will outline these principles and then explain them in more detail.

1. Characteristic Evangelical-Catholic tensions and oppositions which are found together in the life of Israel need to be held together, and this can only be done through a new reception of their roots in the life and Scriptures of Israel.
2. We are to begin from those elements in the life and faith of the other party that are most clearly the work of the Holy Spirit. We are to recognize, honour and as far as possible receive these elements into the life and faith of our own communities.
3. Every step in this process has to be accompanied by a repentance that leads to purification, in particular for all sins of judgment of each other. This repentance is often prompted by the challenge from the Jewish people.
4. We cannot imagine in advance how God will heal our divisions. We have to be prepared for a miracle, not to draw up a programme or a system.

First Principle
Characteristic Evangelical-Catholic tensions and oppositions which are found together in the life of Israel need to be held together.

Once we see that both elements in the tensions and oppositions are complementary in the Israelite-Jewish Scriptures, we know that we have to receive them both, not to choose one at the expense of the other. The big question becomes: how are we to relate these elements: divine initiative and human mediation/instrumentality; spirit and body; word and sacrament/rite; gospel and mystery; freedom and authority; individual and community; Jesus and Mary/saints; Scripture and tradition.

This [holding together] can only be done through a new reception of their roots in the life and Scriptures of Israel.

This right ordering we are to learn from the life and Scriptures of Israel, and from the Holy Spirit. The right ordering means a recognition that in most of these instances, we are not dealing with equals to be carefully balanced. So human instrumentality has to be subordinated to divine initiative and divine revelation. Mary and the saints are subordinated to Jesus Christ. The body receives life from the spirit. Tradition is subordinate to Scripture as the inspired word of God.

The Catholic temptation as the church of tradition is often to forget or minimize the differences between the two elements in each instance, so that the 'and' becomes too much like summer and winter, hot and cold, strawberries and cream. The Evangelical temptation by way of reaction is often to ignore the second element, to eliminate the 'and': God alone, faith alone, word/Bible alone, Jesus alone.

Second Principle

We are to begin from those elements in the life and faith of the other party that are most clearly the work of the Holy Spirit.

Since it is the Holy Spirit that has made these contacts possible, and the respect arising from them, we must look to the Holy Spirit as the basis for these new relationships. We begin therefore from those features in the other party that are most evidently the work of the Holy Spirit.

Often, as the story of M Calisi and G Traettino (page 5 above) makes clear, new doors are opened by unexpected friendships. Such a friendship shows how two men came to respect one another as fellow-Christians and men of God. They saw things in each other that they knew were from God. So, for example, the Catholic sees the Protestant's love for the Scriptures. The Evangelical sees the Catholic's love for Jesus. The Catholic admires the evangelistic zeal of the Evangelical and the commitment to train evangelists. The Evangelical discovers riches in the Catholic heritage of meditation and contemplative prayer.

I recommend seeking ways to experience what is evidently a richness in the other heritage. The Catholic can listen to expository Evangelical preaching that takes the details of the biblical text with great seriousness and reverence. The Evangelical can participate in sung Vespers at a Catholic monastery or read the life of a great Catholic lover of Jesus like Francis of Assisi or Thérèse of Lisieux.

We are to recognize, honour and as far as possible receive these elements into the life and faith of our own communities.

There are steps in this process of growing in knowledge and love of one another:
- First, there is a recognition: this feature is a work of the Holy Spirit.
- Once we recognize something as from the Holy Spirit, we must then honour this feature as a work of the Holy Spirit.

- We should then thank the Lord for this work in the other.
- We need then to ask if there is any way I/we can receive this gift/work of the Spirit into my life/the life of our faith community. Obviously this can only happen as there is certainty about what is of the Spirit, and as there is clarity of ways in which this can be received without denial of our own convictions and distinctive heritage as we have received them from the Lord.

In the elements that we can most easily recognize as the work of the Holy Spirit in the life of the other, we should give a particular place to their heroes of faith and to their martyrs. Each Christian heritage has its share of heroes, those women and men who loved Jesus Christ with their whole hearts. In the 20th century, there have been more Christian martyrs than in all the preceding centuries put together. It is tragic when we know so little of these inspiring stories outside our own traditions. Pope John Paul II has particularly drawn attention to the importance of the martyrs for Christian unity.

Third Principle

Every step in this process has to be accompanied by a repentance that leads to purification, in particular for all sins of judgment of each other.

The steps already indicated in the First and Second Principles call for an appropriate repentance, which is the Christian response to the recognition of sin. As we see that in our faith community we have exaggerated some element and so scandalized other believers or that we have neglected some element of God's truth, maybe by way of reaction, then we should confess this failing, and we should ask God's pardon. In fact, we have mishandled the revelation of God.

Since the replacement thinking lies at the root of our divisions, it is particularly important that we express a repentance for all forms of this error. We will confess our distinctive arrogance, our brand of superiority (Catholics looking down on simplistic, individualistic, fundamentalist Evangelicals; Evangelicals looking down on ignorant, superstitious and priest-ridden Catholics), and every form of judgmentalism.

Fourth Principle

We cannot imagine in advance how God will heal our divisions. We have to be prepared for a miracle, not to draw up a programme or a system.

The bridging of the Evangelical-Catholic chasm is an amazing work of the Holy Spirit. It cannot be planned. It is useless to exercise our imaginations as to how we can be made one. Any attempt to do so will risk alienating the other party, because we cannot avoid bringing in our requirements that have not yet been sufficiently challenged and purified by the Holy Spirit.

We have to guard against all fears, especially the fears that such interaction and fellowship will inevitably compromise our Catholic or our Evangelical faith. The safeguards are provided by the above principles, especially by only advancing through what is clearly biblical in the original 'pre-replacement' sense and through what is undoubtedly of the Holy Spirit. Since the Holy Spirit always glorifies Jesus and leads to worship of Jesus and the Father, to follow these principles will make us all more christocentric, more worship-centred and more Bible-based.